Gilbert **Delahaye** ◆ N

martine

visits the Côte d'Azur

casterman

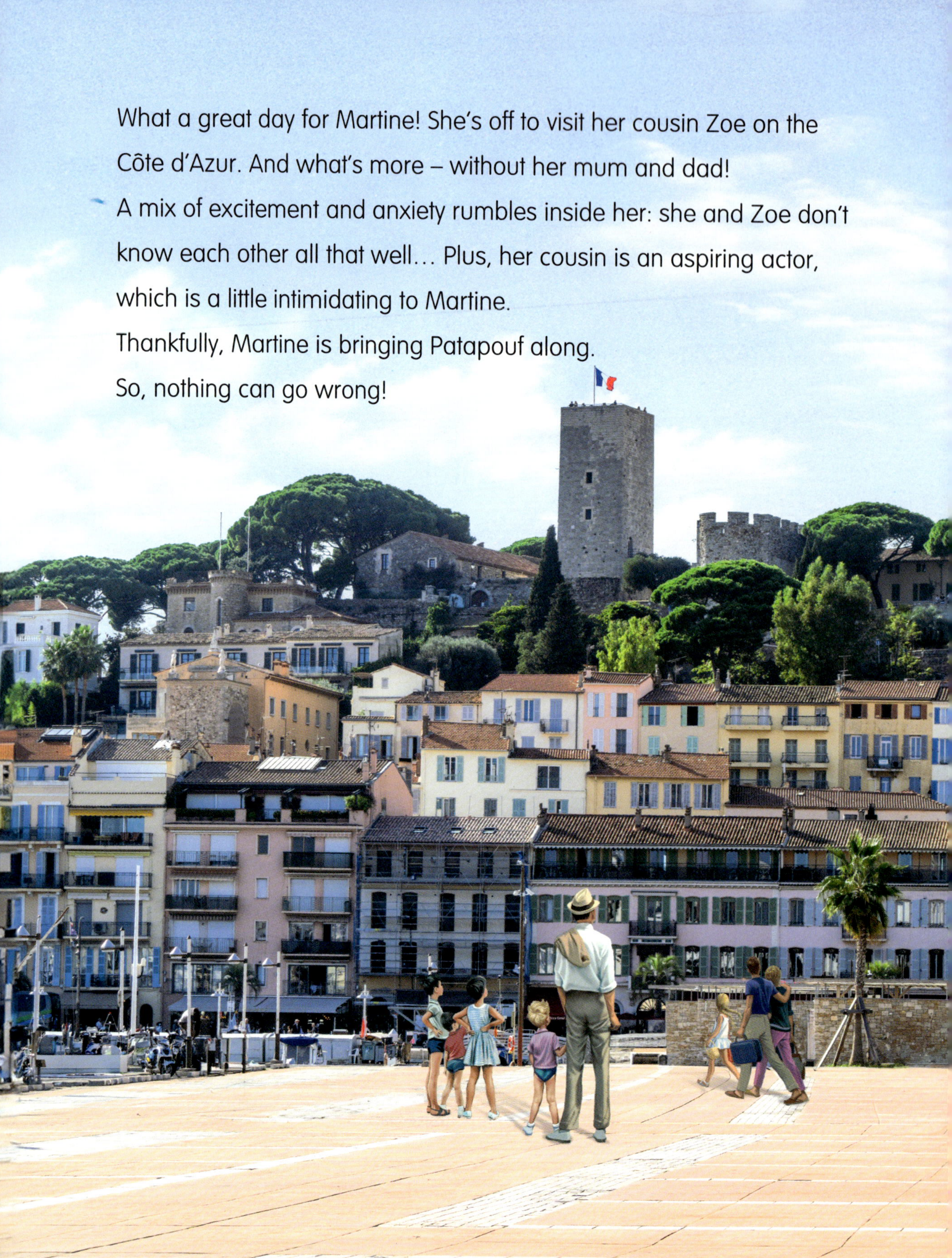

What a great day for Martine! She's off to visit her cousin Zoe on the Côte d'Azur. And what's more – without her mum and dad!

A mix of excitement and anxiety rumbles inside her: she and Zoe don't know each other all that well... Plus, her cousin is an aspiring actor, which is a little intimidating to Martine.

Thankfully, Martine is bringing Patapouf along.

So, nothing can go wrong!

"Welcome to Cannes!" a voice shouts as Martine steps off the train. Zoe greets her on the platform with a grin, alongside her parents, Julia and Sebastien.

"Ready to discover the treasures of the Côte d'Azur?" Sebastien asks. "First of all, we'll drop off your things at home. Then, we can have a walk round Mandelieu."

A few minutes later, the family turns into the Croisette, which runs along the sea.

"How beautiful..." Martine marvels.

While Martine unpacks, Zoe tells her all about an advert she was recently a part of.

"There was a huge crowd of people on the set, and so many cameras!"

"Don't you get stage fright?" Martine asks. "I'd be so nervous!"

Julia interrupts:

"You should get changed, Martine, it's very warm outside. And Zoe, let me button up your dress. And now, off to La Napoule Castle!"

"This place feels like a church..." Martine whispers as they enter the fortress and admire the stained-glass windows and high arches of the dining room.

"... Or like Alice's wonderland!" Zoe adds.

The castle is full of surrealistic engravings and animal statues. Martine draws a few sculptures in her notebook.

As they leave the fortress, Julia's mobile rings.

"Zoe, you won't believe who just called... Marc de la Ruza, the famous director ! He wants you to play in his new film *Princesses of the Côte d'Azur*. What a great opportunity! It's set in the region and the shoot begins tomorrow!"

Martine stops in her tracks.

"What will I do in the meantime?" she asks.

"Come along, of course! It'll be so much fun! Now, there's no time to waste! We must get ready!"

The following morning, Martine, Zoe, Julia and Sebastien set off to Grasse, for the first day of filming. The Place aux Herbes is swarming with camera operators and actors.

"Welcome to the Grasse region!" a man says. "I'm Marc, the director. I'm thrilled to have you on the set. Zoe, go and find the costume designer so you can try on your outfit. As for you, Martine, today while your cousin is shooting, I've signed you up for a very special workshop..."

A few minutes later, Martine enters a bright yellow building.

"Everything here is dedicated to perfume-making," a young woman explains. "And guess what, Martine – you're going to create your own fragrance!"

Martine follows her to a small lab, and takes a seat opposite a display of vials labelled with sensory names: "Menton's lemon", "bergamot", "red mandarin", "neroli"...

Martine leaves the factory two hours later with her very own perfume in hand, for which she has found the perfect name: "Zest of Patapouf"!

The following day, the family heads to Antibes. As they stroll along the coastal path, Zoe talks about her first day of filming.

"And I haven't told you. I get to wear an actual princess dress!"

"Really?" Martine exclaims, astounded.

"I'm sure you could be an extra on the film, you know…"

Martine hadn't thought of that… the prospect seems a bit daunting, but Zoe's enthusiasm is infectious! Martine presses her cousin for more until they reach a creek. Then, the only thing they can think about is… jumping in for a swim!

Marc has agreed to hiring Martine as an extra.
After an hour of fitting, the costume designer decides Martine will wear an orange gown with an elaborate headdress.
"Good luck!" Zoe whispers before her cousin's first take.
As soon as she hears the word "Action!", Martine walks down the central aisle of the Provençal market. She inhales the wonderful smell of lavender, and gazes at the colourful displays of olive bags and spices… The scenery is so captivating that Martine almost forgets the cameras are rolling!

At the end of the day, Marc congratulates Martine:

"Well done! You did a great job today. I'd love for you to carry on."

Martine is so happy with her walk-on part that she promptly accepts.

An old chauffeur-driven convertible provided by the film company takes the family to the next location. Martine and Zoe feel very special!

But, as soon as they arrive, the girls notice the grim look on Marc's face.

"I was expecting a new actress on set today," he explains. "But I've just been told that she's broken her arm. Without her, the shoot can't go on."

This is disastrous news for the crew.

"We should give them some space," Julia decides.

Let's visit Saint-Paul-de-Vence – it's a village of art and history, you know!"

Martine and Zoe are so disappointed that they don't really feel like a cultural tour. But they change their minds as soon as they come across a stunning medieval house…

"What a beautiful place…" Martine exclaims.

"The poet Jacques Prévert lived there for ten years," explains Sebastien.

"They call it La Miette."

"Marc figured out a solution!" Julia tells Zoe and Martine later on that day. "We're to meet him tomorrow in Nice. That's all I know…"

The following day, Marc greets Martine and the rest of the family at the Cours Saleya market.

"Martine, would you be willing to replace the missing actress?"

"Me? How could I? I can't act!"

"And I'm sure you can. So, what do you say?"

Martine did enjoy working as an extra… so why not try something new?

"Okay !" she agrees.

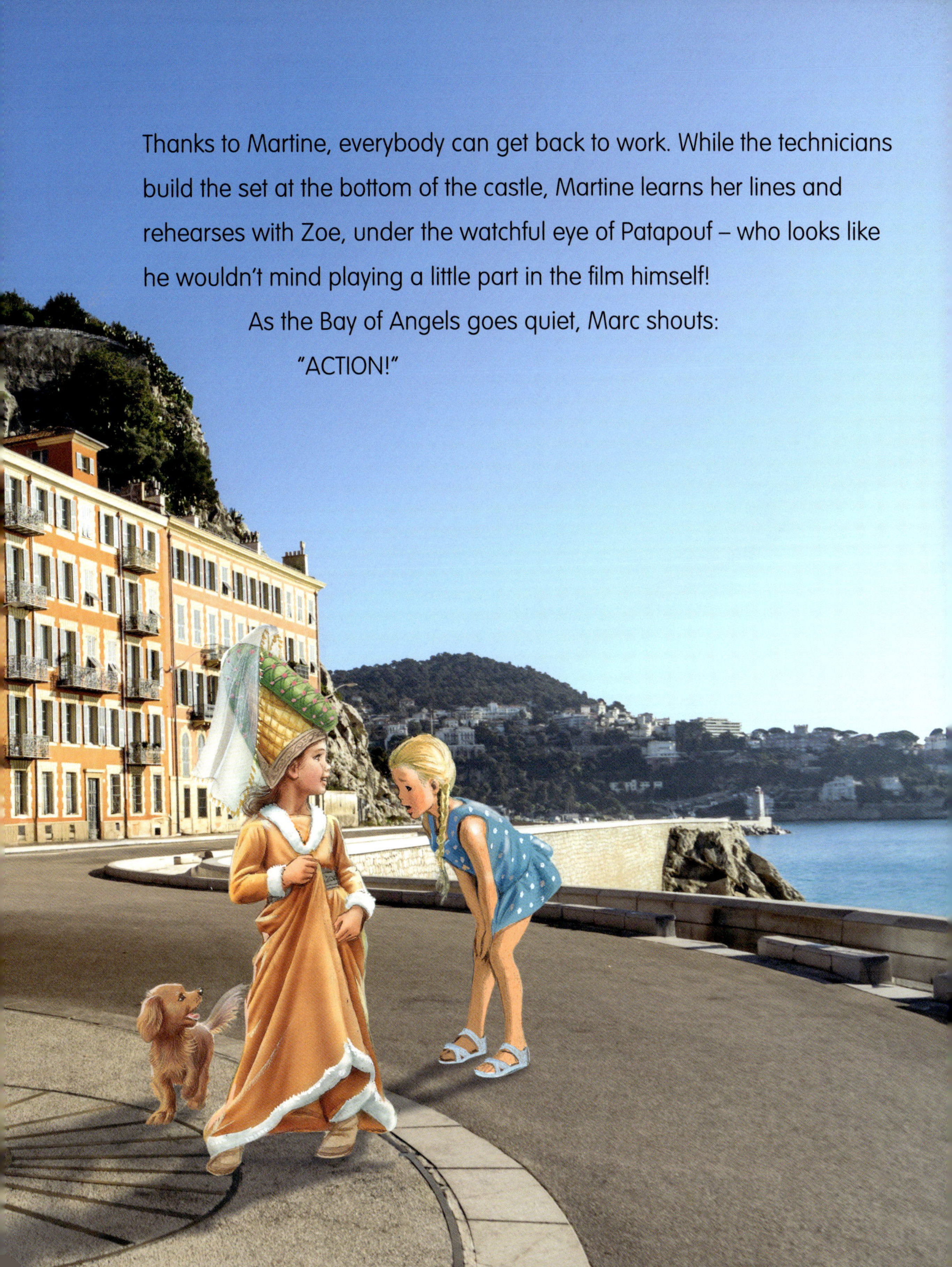

Thanks to Martine, everybody can get back to work. While the technicians build the set at the bottom of the castle, Martine learns her lines and rehearses with Zoe, under the watchful eye of Patapouf – who looks like he wouldn't mind playing a little part in the film himself!

As the Bay of Angels goes quiet, Marc shouts:

"ACTION!"

What an incredible day it's been! With each take, Martine has felt more comfortable, and Marc encouraged her throughout the shoot.
The upcoming scenes are set to take place in the Mercantour park and, over the next few days, the crew share picnic meals in the mountains.
From time to time, they get a visit from a marmot or a chamois.

Acting is amazing – and also exhausting! Martine and Zoe are looking forward to the weekend. "There's plenty to do, here in Valberg, to clear your minds," Sebastien says over breakfast. "You can go hiking, horse riding..."

"Oh, yes! Let's go horse riding!" Martine and Zoe exclaim.

Half an hour later, Martine is seated on the back of a palomino pony.

"Off we go, Socca!" she shouts.

The crew meet up in Menton for the final stretch of filming.

As the technicians get the cameras ready, Martine and Zoe wander around the city and come across a group of petanque players.

"Do you know how to play?" Zoe asks her cousin. "You want to strike that tiny ball over there, called the cochonnet, or at least get as close to it as possible."

"Would you like to show us?" a bearded player asks.

Zoe grabs a big steel ball. She aims and…

"Perfect shot!" the old man exclaims.

The girls would like to play more, but it's time for them to join the crew at the Carnolès palace, a former prince's residence to shoot the only one scene left… the royal ball!

"Hurry up, Martine!" Marc says when she arrives. "Everyone is ready!"

As soon as Martine is in costume, lively music plays out across the citrus garden. Marc does several takes.

At last, he announces happily:

"It's a wrap!" Thank you everyone and see you at the party tonight!

In the meantime, Julia and Sebastien take Martine and Zoe to visit Sainte-Marguerite Island, off the coast of Cannes. As they set out sailing, Julia explains:

"In the 17th century, a prisoner wearing an iron mask was imprisoned in the fort of Sainte-Marguerite. According to some people, he was King Louis XIVth's secret twin brother!"

"That's a dark story..." Martine thinks with a shudder.

Thankfully, looking at the picturesque landscape is enough to cheer her up!

As the sun sets, Martine and Zoe climb a series of winding cobbled lanes leading to the top of Cannes and to Le Suquet, the oldest district of the city. The view is breathtaking…

and the atmosphere positively festive!

"Let's go and dance!" Zoe shouts, grabbing Martine by the hand.

Patapouf seems just as eager to join the fun!

Martine is overwhelmed with pride and happiness as the night falls over Cannes. What an adventure it has been! She travelled to the Côte d'Azur for the first time and found a new passion!

A few months from now, she will attend the premiere of *Princesses of the Côte d'Azur*.

Dreamily, she whispers to Patapouf:

“Suppose they show the film at the Palais des Festivals? I can just see myself walking up the most famous red steps in the world! With you by my side, my darling Patapouf!”

Martine's Journey

The Côte d'Azur

Mandelieu-La Napoule

Blue Mediterranean sea, red Esterel rock massif, yellow flowers all around... the mimosa capital shines in multicoloured ways. Not to mention La Napoule castle, a medieval fortress, bought by American couple Henry and Marie Clews in the 1930s, and its astonishing works of art!

Grasse

So many fragrances float around Grasse! No wonder this 11th century town is considered the world capital of perfume. Alongside the cathedral and the episcopal palace, several famous perfume companies still stand among narrow paved streets. Some of them host workshops where customers can create their own fragrances, like Martine.

Antibes Juan-les-Pins

Surrounded by ramparts, Antibes has been the home of numerous artists throughout the past century: Picasso, Zelda and Francis Scott Fitzgerald, as well as Ray Charles and Ella Fitzgerald, who were great fans of the International jazz Festival and probably also of Antibes's historical centre and beautiful cape!

Saint-Paul-de-Vence

Artists have been attracted to this village since 1920, the "most beautiful light ever", according to Marc Chagall. Art is everywhere in Saint-Paul-de-Vence: here a fountain by George Braque at the Maeght foundation, there collages by Jacques Prévert at "la Colombe d'Or", a stained-glass window by Jean-Michel Folon inside the chapel... and everywhere, cobblestone paving which makes every street a true work of art!

Nice

Before it became famous, the Promenade des Anglais was a simple path drawn in 1822 by Reverend Lewis Way, who wanted to facilitate access to the shore. Nowadays, the Nice carnival on Place Masséna is one of the major events of the city, as well as the Nice flower battle, where decorated floats and 65 feet tall characters parade around the city!

Mercantour National Park

On the border between France and Italy, this natural park extends over... eight valleys! Marmots and chamois can be spotted (with a little luck), as well as mountain goats and a variety of bird species. In 2019, the park was certified as an "International Dark Sky Reserve", making it one of the best places in the world to stargaze on a summer night.

Menton

Menton is the land of lemons, for sure! The Lemon festival was created in 1930 and attracts tens of thousands of visitors every year in February. For the occasion, the town and its numerous gardens adorn themselves with yellow and orange, and floats covered in 150 tonnes of citrus fruit (that's more than 30 elephants!) parade along the streets, to the public's great delight.

Cannes

Red carpet, fine sand, emblematic palaces...
In May, Cannes is transformed into the world's film city, inviting the biggest stars from every continent to climb the steps of the Palais des Festivals. Nature is also cinematic, with the turquoise waters of the Lérins Islands visible from the famous Croisette!

I wish to thank my daughter Eleanor with whom I shared wonderful moments while visiting the Côte d'Azur.
Many thanks also to Laure Toma-Auneau for her warm welcome in Cannes, and for everyone else's hospitality on the Côte d'Azur, especially Franck Raineri from the Grasse tourist information office, Mrs Webster and M. Fabre at the Fragonard historic perfumery.

R. E.-G.

Published in partnership with Côte d'Azur France Tourism board.

Casterman
Rue Haute 139
1000 Bruxelles
Belgique

www.casterman.com

ISBN: 978-2-203-29075-4
Edition number: L.10EJCN000739.N001

Text and translation by Rosalind Elland-Goldsmith
Layout by Neil Desmet
Clipping and map by Nina de Sagazan

Cover: thanyarat07 / istock photo ; Photo12 / Alamy / Endless Travel ; page 3: Hervé Fabre / Palais des Festivals et des Congrès de Cannes ; pages 4 and 5: imantsu / istock photo ; page 6: Hervé Fabre / Palais des Festivals et des Congrès de Cannes ; page 7: Camille Moirenc / OT Mandelieu ; page 8: Flavio Vallenari / istock photo ; page 9: Christian Benoit / OT Pays de Grasse ; page 10: parfumerie Fragonard / Laborant / Shutterstock ; page 11: Photo12 / Alamy / World Pictures / Photoshot, Avalon / World Pictures; page 12: Eddy Galeotti / Shutterstock ; page 13: Freesurf / Adobe Stock ; page 14: SvetlanaSF / Shutterstock ; page 15: Photo12 / Alamy / Kirk Fisher ; pages 16 and 17: Photo12 / Alamy / Francesco Bonino ; page 18: Photo12 / imageBROKER / Egmont Strigl ; page 19: OT Valberg ; pages 20 and 21: Kirk Fisher / Adobe Stock ; page 22: Joëlle Martin / OT Menton ; page 23: Photo12 / Alamy / Chris Hellier ; pages 24 and 25: Fotofantastika / istock photo ; page 26: Zoran Pajic / Shutterstock ; page 27: Camille Moirenc / OT Mandelieu-La Napoule ; OT Grasse ; Côte d'Azur France ; Ruth Peterkin / Shutterstock ; page 28: SvetlanaSF / Shutterstock ; Lionel Lecourtier / Côte d'Azur France ; Joëlle Martin / OT Menton ; Hervé Fabre / Palais des Festivals et des Congrès de Cannes.

Based on Gilbert Delahaye and Marcel Marlier's picture books.
The illustrations are taken and adapted from *Martine au zoo, Martine à la fête des fleurs, Martine prépare une surprise, Martine la leçon de dessin, Martine et le prince mystérieux, Martine et ses amis, les grandes vacances, Martine princesses et chevaliers, Martine protège la nature, Martine un amour de poney* and *Anne et Françoise en vacances*.

Printed in February 2025, in France, by PPO Graphic
(10 rue de la Croix Martre, 91120 Palaiseau).
Legal deposit: April 2025 ; D.2025/0053/44
Deposited at the Ministry of Justice, Paris (law n°49.956 of July 16, 1949, on publications aimed at young people)